The Urbana Free Library

To renew: call **217-367-4057**
or go to **urbanafreelibrary.org**
and select **My Account**

OOPS! THEY'RE MICROWAVES!

BY NICK WOJTON

Gareth Stevens
PUBLISHING

Please visit our website, www.garethstevens.com. For a free color catalog of all our high-quality books, call toll free 1-800-542-2595 or fax 1-877-542-2596.

Cataloging-in-Publication Data

Names: Wojton, Nick.
Title: Oops! they're microwaves! / Nick Wojton.
Description: New York : Gareth Stevens Publishing, 2020. | Series: Accidental scientific discoveries that changed the world | Includes glossary and index.
Identifiers: ISBN 9781538239988 (pbk.) | ISBN 9781538240007 (library bound) | ISBN 9781538239995 (6 pack)
Subjects: LCSH: Microwaves–Juvenile literature. | Microwave ovens–Juvenile literature. | Spencer, Percy, 1894-1970–Juvenile literature.
Classification: LCC TK7876.W658 2020 | DDC 621.381'3–dc23

First Edition

Published in 2020 by
Gareth Stevens Publishing
111 East 14th Street, Suite 349
New York, NY 10003

Copyright © 2020 Gareth Stevens Publishing

Designer: Katelyn E. Reynolds
Editor: Monika Davies

Photo credits: Cover, p. 1 arka38/Shutterstock.com; cover, pp. 1–32 (burst) jirawat phueksriphan/Shutterstock.com; cover, pp. 1–32 (burst lines) KID_A/Shutterstock.com; p. 5 Africa Studio/Shutterstock.com; p. 7 VectorMine/Shutterstock.com; p. 8 Retrieved March 21, 2015 from Short Wave Craft magazine, Popular Book Corp., New York, Vol. 4, No. 7, November 1933, p. 394 (http://www.americanradiohistory.com/Archive-Short-Wave-Television/30s/SW-TV-1933-11.pdf)/Chetvorno/Wikipedia.org; pp. 9, 19 Designua/Shutterstock.com; p. 11 Crown/Mirrorpix/Mirrorpix via Getty Images; p. 13 SSPL/Getty Images; p. 15 Andriana Syvanych/Shutterstock.com; p. 17 Acroterion/Wikipedia.org; p. 21 ML Harris/Shutterstock.com; p. 23 vvoe/Shutterstock.com; p. 25 Shkliarov/Shutterstock.com; p. 27 Andrea Rugg/Corbis Documentary/Getty Images; p. 29 Pictorial Parade/Archive Photos/Getty Images.

Printed in the United States of America

CPSIA compliance information: Batch #CS19GS: For further information contact Gareth Stevens, New York, New York at 1-800-542-2595.

CONTENTS

Words in the glossary appear in **bold** type the first time they are used in the text.

READY IN MINUTES

Are you short on time and feeling hungry? You might head to the kitchen and warm up a meal using a familiar **appliance**. Making a fast snack is easy thanks to an everyday kitchen item: the microwave oven. Just hit a few buttons on one, and a quick meal is ready for you to eat!

However, the microwave oven hasn't always been a part of the kitchen. Before its invention, you'd use a hotplate or frying pan to warm up your food. It wasn't until 1946 that the world met its first microwave oven. And, this invention was made possible with an accidental discovery.

Stovetop Living

BEFORE MICROWAVES, THE FASTEST WAY TO WARM UP OR COOK A MEAL WAS USING THE STOVE. THIS APPLIANCE HAS BEEN AROUND FOR CENTURIES. ANCIENT EGYPTIANS AND OTHER ANCIENT CIVILIZATIONS USED STONE AND BRICK STOVES TO COOK MEALS. PEOPLE STILL USE STOVES FOR COOKING, BUT THEY'RE NOT AS QUICK FOR WARMING UP AN ALREADY COOKED ITEM.

Around 90 percent of all US households have a microwave oven in their kitchen.

5

MICROWAVE OVENS VS. MICROWAVES

When you think of a microwave, you probably picture the microwave oven sitting in your kitchen. However, the word "microwave" has another meaning!

A microwave is also a wave of energy. These waves of energy are similar to light but unable to be seen by the human eye. A wave of energy can transmit, or pass on, energy, which is power used to do work. Light, sound, and electrical are all types of energy.

Microwaves can transmit heat energy. Transmitting heat energy to an item will usually increase the temperature of the item, making it hotter. In a microwave oven, microwaves transmit heat energy to the item inside the oven.

ELECTROMAGNETIC RADIATION

MICROWAVES ARE A TYPE OF ELECTROMAGNETIC **RADIATION**. THESE ARE ENERGY WAVES THAT ARE PART ELECTRIC AND PART MAGNETIC. THESE WAVES CAN MOVE THROUGH SPACE AT THE SPEED OF LIGHT—WHICH IS FASTER THAN THE EYE CAN SEE! THERE ARE SEVEN TYPES OF ELECTROMAGNETIC RADIATION. EACH ONE IS USED FOR DIFFERENT PURPOSES.

Each type of electromagnetic radiation has a different-sized wavelength. Microwaves have the second-longest wavelength.

THE SEVEN TYPES OF ELECTROMAGNETIC RADIATION

| RADIO | MICROWAVES | INFRARED | VISIBLE LIGHT | ULTRAVIOLET | X-RAYS | GAMMA |

When microwaves are aimed at food, the water molecules, or very small pieces of matter, in the food twist very quickly. While twisting, the molecules push against each other, creating **friction**. This produces heat, which in turn, heats or cooks the food.

There are three reasons why microwaves can be used to heat and cook food. First, microwaves **reflect** off metal, including the metal walls inside a microwave oven. Second, microwaves can go through glass, paper, and plastic. Third, food items can absorb, or take in, microwaves. This means plastic or glass **containers** won't absorb microwaves, but they can heat or cook food held in containers made of these materials.

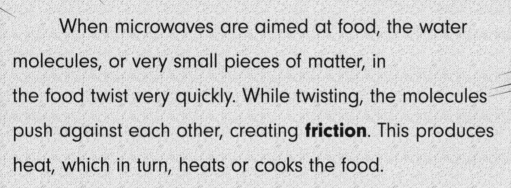

1933 WORLD'S FAIR

PREHISTORIC MICROWAVE OVEN

BEFORE THE INVENTION OF THE MICROWAVE OVEN, PEOPLE HAD ALREADY TRIED USING RADIO WAVES TO HEAT FOOD. AT THE 1933 WORLD'S FAIR IN CHICAGO, THE WESTINGHOUSE COMPANY ATTACHED TWO RADIO **TRANSMITTERS** TO TWO METAL PLATES. THEN, THEY PLACED A STEAK WITH POTATOES BETWEEN THE TWO PLATES. RADIO WAVES WERE SENT BETWEEN THE TWO PLATES, HEATING THE FOOD.

HEATING
WITH
MICROWAVES

WATER MOLECULES TWISTING

The microwaves in a microwave oven can heat a food item quicker than the heating system in a conventional, or standard, oven. Microwaves can travel through a food item, so it can heat both the inside and outside at the same time.

SPENCER'S SPECTACULAR SNACK DISCOVERY

In the 1940s, radio waves and microwaves were used—but not for cooking and heating food. These energy waves were an important part of radars, or machines that use microwaves and radio waves to locate and identify objects. During World War II, radars were used to track enemy airplanes.

Percy Spencer, an American **engineer** working at Raytheon Company, was part of a team creating radars for the war. In 1945, Spencer was looking around one of the company's laboratories. A peanut cluster bar was tucked in his pocket. He had no idea the snack he was saving for later would lead to an accidental discovery.

A Self-Taught Engineer

Born in 1894, Percy Spencer began putting in electricity at a paper mill at the age of 14. He later joined the US Navy. When Spencer wasn't working, he was studying, and he taught himself as much as he could about the latest scientific discoveries. By the 1920s, he'd become a leading EXPERT on radars.

This man worked at a ground control center that used radars to spy enemy airplanes in World War II. Radars could pinpoint the location of incoming enemy airplanes from hundreds of miles away!

That day, Spencer paused to look at an active, or working, magnetron in a radar. He'd been trying to improve the magnetron, which is a closed **vacuum** tube that produces microwaves. The magnetron was a key part of radars.

While standing next to the magnetron, Spencer stuck his hand in his pocket. However, instead of finding his peanut cluster bar, he discovered it had melted! "It was a gooey, sticky mess," Spencer later remembered. He started to wonder if the microwaves from the magnetron had melted his peanut cluster bar. Spencer realized that if this was the case, microwaves in a closed container could possibly heat food.

CHOCOLATE OR PEANUT BAR?

OVER TIME, THE KEY INGREDIENT IN PERCY SPENCER'S FAMOUS DISCOVERY HAS CHANGED. SOME HAVE SAID IT WAS A CHOCOLATE BAR IN HIS POCKET. HOWEVER, SPENCER'S GRANDSON CLAIMS HIS GRANDFATHER LIKELY HAD A PEANUT CLUSTER BAR IN HIS POCKET. PERCY SPENCER WAS A NATURE LOVER AND SOMETIMES FED THE SQUIRRELS OUTSIDE WITH PEANUT BARS.

Built in 1940, this original cavity magnetron powered radars used in World War II. This magnetron led to the future version of the magnetron used in microwave ovens today.

EGG-CELLENT EXPERIMENTS

Spencer decided to test a few other foods. He fired up the radar once again. Then, he put popcorn kernels next to the radar—and watched the kernels pop open all over the laboratory!

Spencer's most famous, or well-known, experiment to test his microwave **theory** involved an egg. Some of Spencer's fellow engineers were doubtful microwaves could heat food. To prove his theory, Spencer cut a hole in a kettle and placed an egg inside. He then aimed microwaves at the egg. As the story goes, one engineer got too close to the kettle—and the egg exploded all over him!

14

PATENTING THE PROCESS

ON OCTOBER 8, 1945, SPENCER FILED FOR A PATENT THAT GAVE HIM THE RIGHTS TO THE MICROWAVE COOKING METHOD. A PATENT IS AN OFFICIAL DOCUMENT THAT GIVES A PERSON THE RIGHTS TO A DESIGN, MACHINE, OR PROCESS FOR A TIME. HIS PATENT, TITLED "METHOD OF TREATING FOODSTUFFS," WAS GRANTED TO HIM ON JANUARY 24, 1950.

Spencer's patent, "Method of Treating Foodstuffs", included diagrams of how microwaves could be used to make popcorn!

15

MASSIVE MICROWAVES

Soon after his discovery, Spencer and other Raytheon workers designed the first closed-box type of microwave oven. This oven included a magnetron that produced microwaves. However, the first microwave ovens were too big. The model, named the Radarange, was nearly 6 feet (1.8 m) tall and weighed over 700 pounds (317.5 kg)!

The Radarange hit the market in 1947. Due to their large size, the first microwave ovens were mainly used in places that made food for large groups, such as on ships and at restaurants. These microwave ovens were also expensive, costing nearly $3,000. It wasn't until the late 1960s that microwaves started to become smaller, cheaper, and a common part of home kitchens.

Sizing Down

IN 1967, THE RAYTHEON-OWNED COMPANY, AMANA, RELEASED A MUCH SMALLER MICROWAVE OVEN. THIS MICROWAVE OVEN HAD A NEW—AND CHEAPER—VARIATION OF THE MAGNETRON THAT HAD BEEN DEVELOPED IN JAPAN. THIS NEW MICROWAVE OVEN WAS MEANT TO SIT ON COUNTERTOPS. HOWEVER, THIS VERSION STILL COST ALMOST $500!

24
Radar
Range

In the 1950s, the NS *Savannah*, a US Navy ship, received a Radarange. While a large, bulky item, the Radarange fit right in with its surroundings while aboard a clunky, metal ship.

MICROWAVE OVEN 101

Microwave ovens have gotten smaller over the years, but they have many elements from the first ones. A magnetron still sits behind the strong walls of today's microwave ovens. The magnetron is a key part of the microwave oven, as it **converts** electricity from the wall plug into microwaves. The microwaves are then pumped into the box of the oven through an antenna, or metal rod or wire.

Inside the oven's box, microwaves bounce around and through your food. Remember how microwaves can excite the water molecules in food? This process is called radiation heating, which is how your food becomes nice and hot.

MAGNETRON MAGIC

A FILAMENT, OR THIN-THREADLIKE OBJECT, SITS IN THE MIDDLE OF THE MAGNETRON. THIS FILAMENT IS HEATED UP AND GIVES OFF ELECTRONS. THE ELECTRONS BUILD UP AND FLY BETWEEN TWO POWERFUL MAGNETS PLACED ON OPPOSITE SIDES OF A VACUUM TUBE. MICROWAVES ARE CREATED FROM THIS FLOW OF ELECTRONS, WHICH ARE THEN PUSHED INTO THE MICROWAVE OVEN'S BOX.

PARTS OF A MICROWAVE OVEN

The transformer is another important part of the microwave oven. The standard household electrical outlet voltage is 120 volts. The transformer converts this voltage to over 4,000 volts to power the magnetron.

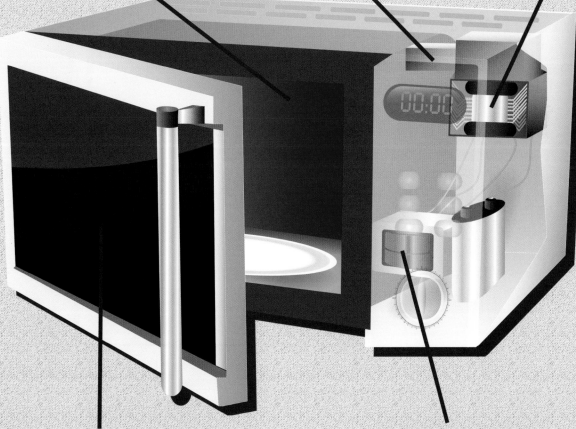

COOKING CHAMBER

ANTENNA

MAGNETRON

METAL MESH DOOR

TRANSFORMER

Every microwave oven also includes strong, metal walls within the oven's box. Microwaves can't go through these walls. Instead, the microwaves are trapped inside and reflect off the walls, similar to how light reflects off a mirror. The trapped microwaves keep constantly heating your food.

The door on a microwave oven is designed with safety in mind. There is a metal mesh on the door, which is made of small holes. This metal mesh allows visible light to escape the microwave oven, letting us see inside the microwave oven. However, the holes in the metal mesh are small enough that microwaves can't get out.

EQUAL TURNTABLES

MOST MICROWAVE OVENS ALSO INCLUDE A GLASS TURNTABLE THAT SITS AT THE BOTTOM OF THE BOX. THIS TURNTABLE TURNS YOUR FOOD ITEMS IN A CIRCULAR MOTION. AS MICROWAVES BOUNCE AROUND IN THE OVEN, THERE ARE AREAS IN THE OVEN THAT ARE HOTTER OR COLDER THAN OTHERS. A TURNTABLE HELPS MAKE SURE YOUR FOOD IS EVENLY COOKED OR HEATED.

While many people use their microwave oven to reheat leftovers, you can also use it to cook meals and desserts, such as pasta and brownies.

SAFETY FIRST

Microwave ovens are safe appliances. However, the ovens do produce microwave radiation, which, in high levels, can be dangerous. In the United States, there are regulations, or rules, that ensure microwave ovens can't leak enough dangerous radiation to cause harm to humans. Microwave ovens are built so they only produce microwaves when the oven is turned on and the door is fully closed. The chances of getting a radiation-related injury are very slim.

Most injuries caused by a microwave oven happen for a different reason. Liquids and foods can heat to extremely high temperatures in a microwave oven. This can cause extreme burns if these food items are not handled properly. Be careful!

Microwave Metal? Nope!

IT'S BEST NOT TO PUT METAL OBJECTS, LIKE KNIVES OR FORKS, INSIDE YOUR MICROWAVE OVEN. WHILE MICROWAVES ARE ABSORBED BY FOOD ITEMS, MICROWAVES REFLECT OFF METAL OBJECTS. IF THERE ISN'T AN ITEM IN THE OVEN THAT CAN ABSORB THE REFLECTED MICROWAVES, THE METAL OBJECT MAY SPARK UP, CAUSING HARM TO THE OVEN.

Safety devices are built into microwave oven doors to keep the door firmly shut. US regulations state that two of these safety devices must be included in every microwave oven.

EFFICIENT AND EFFECTIVE

Microwave ovens have made cooking and heating food a quick and easy task. However, some believe that microwaves can have side effects on your food. People have wondered if microwaves destroy important **nutrients** in foods, such as vegetables.

Some nutrients do break down when exposed to heat. However, compared to other types of ovens, microwave ovens use less heat and cook food items much faster. Nutrients in your food are therefore exposed to less heat than in most other ovens. One study showed that spinach cooked in a microwave kept 77 percent more of its nutrients than when it was cooked on a stove.

Vegetable Vitamins

USING WATER TO HEAT UP VEGETABLES CAN TAKE OUT THE VEGETABLES' IMPORTANT NUTRIENTS. WHEN BOILED, THE **VITAMINS** IN VEGETABLES CAN LEAK OUT INTO THE WATER. HOWEVER, A MICROWAVE OVEN CAN HEAT UP VEGETABLES USING LITTLE TO NO WATER. THIS IS A GOOD WAY TO KEEP HEALTHY VITAMINS IN YOUR VEGETABLES.

While it's a good idea to use a microwave oven to heat up most vegetables, cauliflower should stay off the list. This vegetable has been shown to lose a larger amount of vitamins when microwaved.

Since the first model, the microwave oven has come a long way. Once, the massive microwave oven could barely fit through a kitchen door. Now, microwave ovens can sit neatly in a kitchen corner. And, in recent years, they have come to include different gears and gadgets.

Many microwave ovens now have settings to cook specific foods, such as popcorn. Knobbed spin timers on ovens have been mostly replaced by digital timers. Some microwave ovens are now built into kitchen walls. The microwave oven continues to make cooking certain meals and heating up leftovers a faster—and easier—experience.

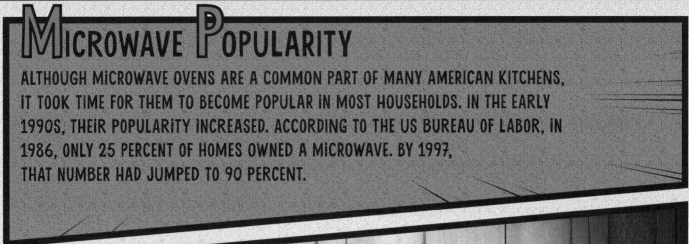

MICROWAVE POPULARITY

ALTHOUGH MICROWAVE OVENS ARE A COMMON PART OF MANY AMERICAN KITCHENS, IT TOOK TIME FOR THEM TO BECOME POPULAR IN MOST HOUSEHOLDS. IN THE EARLY 1990S, THEIR POPULARITY INCREASED. ACCORDING TO THE US BUREAU OF LABOR, IN 1986, ONLY 25 PERCENT OF HOMES OWNED A MICROWAVE. BY 1997, THAT NUMBER HAD JUMPED TO 90 PERCENT.

Microwave ovens used to always sit on kitchen countertops. Now, microwave ovens sometimes hang above stovetops, taking up much less space in the kitchen.

A BRIGHT FUTURE

The microwave oven remains a popular kitchen appliance. So, what exactly could the future hold for the microwave? Upcoming products could be smarter and smaller. For example, there's now a microwave oven that is small enough to fit in your backpack. It can be used while you're on the go!

Without the invention of the microwave oven, we might still be using more trying and time-consuming methods to cook the simplest of foods. The microwave oven has changed cooking in the kitchen forever—and its invention was all thanks to the accidental melting of a candy bar!

A Well-Deserved Honor

THE NATIONAL INVENTORS HALL OF FAME HONORS AND RECOGNIZES FAMOUS INVENTORS, SUCH AS THOMAS EDISON, WHO INVENTED THE ELECTRIC LAMP. IN 1999, NEARLY 30 YEARS AFTER HIS DEATH, PERCY SPENCER WAS INDUCTED INTO THE HALL OF FAME FOR HIS WORK WITH MAGNETRONS, WHICH LED TO HIS INVENTION OF THE MICROWAVE OVEN.

This 1958 advertisement featured one of the early microwave oven models, which was bigger than most modern kitchen ovens!

GLOSSARY

appliance: a machine that uses electricity and is found in people's houses to perform a certain job

container: an object used to hold something

convert: to cause to change form

engineer: someone who plans and builds machines

expert: someone who knows a great deal about something

friction: the force that slows motion between two objects touching each other

nutrient: something a living thing needs to grow and stay alive

radiation: waves of energy

reflect: to throw back light, heat, or sound

theory: an explanation based on facts that is generally accepted by scientists

transmitter: a device that sends out radio waves

vacuum: an empty space without any matter in it

vitamin: a natural matter that is often found in foods and helps a body be healthy

voltage: a measurement of electrical energy

wavelength: amount of space between one energy wave and the next.

FOR MORE INFORMATION

BOOKS

Higgins, Nadia. *Fun Food Inventions.* Minneapolis, MN: Lerner Publications Company, 2014.

Latta, Sara L. *Microwave Man: Percy Spencer and His Sizzling Invention.* Berkeley Heights, NJ: Enslow Elementary, 2014.

Nydal Dahl, Øyvind. *Electronics for Kids: Play with Simple Circuits and Experiment with Electricity!* San Francisco, CA: No Starch Press, 2016.

WEBSITES

The Electromagnetic Spectrum
imagine.gsfc.nasa.gov/science/toolbox/emspectrum1.html
Learn more about the electromagnetic spectrum.

What is a Microwave Oven?
mocomi.com/microwave-ovens
Find out more about the science behind microwave ovens.

Why Can't Metal Objects Go in the Microwave?
wonderopolis.org/wonder/why-cant-metal-objects-go-in-the-microwave
Discover why metal isn't microwavable.

INDEX